南無本師釋迦牟尼佛

宣公上人德相

慈悲普度信者得救成正覺
過化存神禮之獲福悟無生

The Venerable Master Hsuan Hua
His kindness and compassion cross over all; Believers are liberated and perfect the Right Enlightenment.
Transforming beings wherever he goes, his spirit remains intact;
Those who venerate him obtain blessings and awaken to the Unproduced.

為什麼要受持五戒？

Why should we receive and uphold the Five Precepts?

為什麼要受持五戒？

宣化上人講述

英譯
佛經翻譯委員會

出版
佛經翻譯委員會
法界佛教大學
法界佛教總會
美國・加州・柏林根市

Why should we receive and uphold the Five Precepts?

Talks given by Venerable Master
Hsuan Hua

English translation by the
Buddhist Text Translation Society

Buddhist Text Translation Society
Dharma Realm Buddhist University
Dharma Realm Buddhist Association
Burlingame, CA U.S.A.

Published and translated by:
Buddhist Text Translation Society
1777 Murchison Drive
Burlingame, CA 94010-4504

© 2001 Buddhist Text Translation Society
　　　　Dharma Realm Buddhist University
　　　　Dharma Realm Buddhist Association

First bilingual edition 2001

Printed in Taiwan

Library of Congress Cataloging-in-Publication Data
Hsuan Hua, 1908-
　　[Wei shi mo yao shou chi wu jie English]
　　Why should we receive and uphold the five precepts?/ talks given by Venerable Master Hsuan Hua; English translation by the Buddhist Text Translation Society.
　　　　p. cm.
　　English and Chinese.
　　ISBN 0-88139-510-2
　　1. Five Precepts (Buddhism) I. Title: Wei shi mo yao shou chi wu jie. II Buddhist Text Translation Society. III. Title.
　　BQ5495 .H75 2001
　　294.3'5–dc21　　　　　　　　　　　　　　　　　　　　2001025870

Notes: Pinyin is used for the romanization of Chinese words, except for proper names which retain familiar romanizations.

Addresses of the Dharma Realm Buddhist Association's branch offices are listed at the back of this book.

佛經翻譯要員會八項基本守則
The Eight Guidelines of the Buddhist Text Translation Society

1. 從事翻譯工作者不得抱有個人的名利。
   A volunteer must free him/herself from the motives of personal fame and reputation.

2. 從事翻譯工作者不得貢高我慢,必須以虔誠恭敬的態度來工作。
   A volunteer must cultivate a sincere and respectful attitude free from arrogance and conceit.

3. 從事翻譯工作者不得自讚毀他。
   A volunteer must refrain from aggrandizing his/her work and denigrating that of others.

4. 從事翻譯工作者不得自以為是,對他人作品吹毛求疵。
   A volunteer must not establish him/herself as the standard of correctness and suppress the work of others with his or her fault-finding.

5. 從事翻譯工作者必須以佛心為己心。
   A volunteer must take the Buddha-mind as his/her own mind.

6. 從事翻譯工作者必須運用擇法眼來辨別正確的道理。
   A volunteer must use the wisdom of Dharma-Selecting Vision to determine true principles.

7. 從事翻譯工作者必須懇請十方大德長老來印證其翻譯。
   A volunteer must request Virtuous Elders in the ten directions to certify his/her translations.

8. 從事翻譯工作者之作品在獲得印證之後,必須努力弘揚流通經、律、論以及佛書以光大佛教。
   A volunteer must endeavor to propagate the teachings by printing Sutras, Shastra texts, and Vinaya texts when the translations are certified as being correct.

目錄

不要錯過受五戒的機會 2

什麼叫「居士」? 8

什麼叫「五戒」? 10

什麼叫「十善」? 12

什麼叫「綺語」? 14

十善是什麼? 16

必須向出家人求戒 18

佛教徒要守持的根本戒律 20

可不可以抽菸? 28

受五戒的重要性 34

受五戒的好處 42

學佛法沒有什麼利益? 56

不受戒是真「自由」嗎? 60

學佛法就要學戒、定、慧。 64

老修行的故事 66

文殊菩薩的寶珠 70

CONTENTS

Don't miss the chance to receive the five precepts 3

Who are lay people? 9

What are the five precepts? 11

What are the ten good deeds? 13

What is loose speech? 15

What are the ten good deeds? 17

Precepts should be requested from a
      left-home person--an ordained monk 19

The basic rules to be observed by Buddhists 21

Is smoking allowed? 29

The importance of receiving the five precepts 35

The benefits of receiving the five precepts 43

Is there no benefit in studying the Buddhadharma? 57

Will not receiving precepts give you true freedom? 61

In learning Buddhadharma, we must learn precepts,
      concentration, and wisdom. 65

The story of an old cultivator 67

Mañjuśrī Bodhisattva's precious pearl 71

不要做自己的辯護律師　74
什麼是淨戒？　78

Don't act as your own defense attorney **75**
What are pure precepts? **79**

開經偈

無上甚深微妙法
百千萬劫難遭遇
我今見聞得受持
願解如來真實義

VERSE FOR OPENING A SUTRA

The unsurpassed, deep, profound, subtle,
   wonderful Dharma,
In hundreds of thousands of millions of
   eons, is difficult to encounter;
I now see and hear it,
   receive and uphold it,
And I vow to fathom the Tathagata's
   true and actual meaning.

不要錯過受五戒的機會

受五戒、八戒的人,都叫「優婆塞」、「優婆夷」,受過菩薩戒,就叫「菩薩」。本來只有出家人受菩薩戒,但因菩薩是自利利人的,所以在家人也可以受菩薩戒。

在佛教,受戒是很要緊的,想受戒的人,不要錯過機會。

你受一戒也可以,受兩戒也可以,受三戒也可以,受四戒、五戒也可以,受八戒也可以,但是不能受十戒;在

DON'T MISS THE CHANCE TO RECEIVE THE FIVE PRECEPTS

People who receive the five precepts, or the eight precepts, are called *Upasaka* (for men) or *Upasika* (for women). If they take the Bodhisattva precepts then they are called Bodhisattvas of initial resolve, because they are making a commitment to uphold the Bodhisattva precepts and follow the Bodhisattva path. Left-home people receive and uphold the Bodhisattva precepts. But since Bodhisattvas of initial resolve are people who wish to learn how to benefit both themselves and others, lay people, too, can receive lay Bodhisattva precepts.

In Buddhism, receiving and upholding precepts is very important. When there is an opportunity to do so, people should not miss the opportunity

A person can receive one precept, two precepts, three precepts, four precepts, or five precepts. He can also

家人不能受十戒,十戒是沙彌戒,可以受菩薩戒,十重四十八輕戒。

受一戒叫「少份戒」;
受兩戒叫「半份戒」;
受三戒叫「多份戒」;
受五戒叫「全份戒」。

譬如你不能不殺生,不能戒殺戒,你可以受不偷盜的戒。你歡喜飲酒,好像我有個酒徒弟,不願受「酒」戒,你不受酒戒可以受其他的戒。「我喜歡講大話,這個『妄語戒』我不能受。」你可以受其他四戒。「我不能受殺戒,有時候螞蟻小蚊蟲,在無意中我會傷了牠們的生命。如果受戒再犯戒,那更有罪了。」那你可以不受殺生戒,這隨你自己的意思。受一戒、

receive the eight precepts but he is not eligible to receive the ten precepts, as those are reserved for *shramaneras* (novice monks) and *shramanerikas* (novice nuns). But you can take the Bodhisattva precepts, the ten major and forty-eight minor precepts.

> *Receiving one precept is called taking*
>   *"a minimum share of the precepts,"*
> *Receiving two precepts is called taking*
>   *"a half share of the precepts,"*
> *Receiving three precepts is called taking*
>   *"a majority share of the precepts,"*
> *Receiving five precepts is called taking*
>   *"a full share of the precepts."*

If someone has a problem with receiving the precept of not killing beings, then that person can refrain from receiving that precept and can receive the precept of not stealing. If someone likes to drink, like my wine-drinking disciple who didn't want to take the precept prohibiting the consuming of intoxicants, then that person can refrain from receiving the precept prohibiting the consumption of intoxicants, but can receive the others.

兩戒、三戒、五戒都可以,不要錯過這個機會!

在中國受戒,你沒有二百塊錢(美金),你受不了的。那個錢不是做縵衣的錢;縵衣袍是要你自己做,那做多少錢不管你。你歡喜做好一點就用多點錢,你想做不好的就用少點錢。你就單單受戒,供養師父及供養廟上,這兩百塊也不算多的。

Someone may say, "I like to boast. I cannot receive the precept against lying." Well, that person can receive the other four precepts.

Another person may say, "I cannot promise not to kill. Sometimes, unintentionally, I may kill ants and small bugs. If I kill them after receiving the precepts, my offenses will be greater." That person doesn't have to receive the precept against killing. In general, each person can do whatever he or she prefers, receiving one, two, three, or up to five precepts. Just don't miss this opportunity.

In China, if a person cannot afford to pay (it used to cost two hundred US dollars), then he won't be able to receive the precepts. That money did not go toward the purchase of a sash and robe. The preceptees had to purchase those items by themselves. They could buy better or lesser quality sashes and robes, depending on what they had to spend. Just to receive the precepts, one had to make an offering to the teacher and his temple of at least two hundred dollars.

什麼叫「居士」?

什麼叫「居士」?居士,就是居家修道之士,也就是在家相信佛法的人,守持五戒奉行十善的人就叫居士。

WHO ARE LAY PEOPLE?

A layperson is someone who believes in Buddhism, upholds the five precepts, and practices the ten good deeds and who has not left the home-life.

什麼叫「五戒」？

就是殺、盜、婬、妄、酒,五種戒。現在有很多人受過五戒了,這都叫居士了。

WHAT ARE THE FIVE PRECEPTS?

They are the precepts against killing, stealing, engaging in sexual misconduct, and taking intoxicants. People who have received the five precepts are called lay people.

什麼叫「十善」？

十善是十惡的反面。十惡是什麼呢？身有三惡－－殺、盜、婬。意有三惡－－貪、瞋、癡。口有四惡－－綺語、妄言、惡口、兩舌，幾乎佔了十惡的一半。

WHAT ARE THE TEN GOOD DEEDS?

The ten good deeds are just the opposite of ten bad deeds. The ten bad deeds are: killing, stealing, and sexual misconduct, which are done by the body; greed, hatred, and ignorance, which belong to the mind; and lying, loose speech, harsh speech, and divisive speech, which are committed by the mouth. Notice that the offenses of the mouth account for almost half of the ten.

什麼叫「綺語」?

說話非常不正當,有的說某某女人如何如何,或者說某家如何如何,綺語所說的話近於邪,不正當的話。

「妄言」就是打妄語。

「惡口」就是罵人,罵人就是造口業。

「兩舌」,一個人怎麼會長兩個舌頭呢?這不是生了兩個舌頭,是這個人說兩種話,對甲就說乙如何如何,再對乙說甲如何如何,互相挑撥離間,這就是兩舌。

WHAT IS LOOSE SPEECH?

Loose speech is crude or lewd speech, such as talking about how women (or men) behave, or gossiping, and so forth.

Lying means not telling the truth.

Harsh speech refers to scolding people, which creates mouth karma.

Divisive speech means being double-tongued in the sense that one backbites and causes schisms. Such a person tells A about B and then B about A, trying to split them up. That is how divisive speech works.

十善是什麼？

十惡反過來就是十善。十善是什麼？就是不殺生、不偷盜、不邪婬、不貪、不瞋、不癡、不綺語、不妄語、不惡口、不兩舌。這個惡，你不做了，就是善。居士要守五戒行十善。

WHAT ARE THE TEN GOOD DEEDS?

Turn the ten evil deeds around and they become the ten good deeds. What are the ten good deeds? They are: not killing, not stealing, not indulging in sexual misconduct, not being greedy, not harboring hatred, not being deluded, not using loose speech, not lying, not saying harsh words, and not engaging in divisive speech. If you can refrain from doing all these bad things, then you will be wholesome. Lay people should practice these ten good deeds. All lay people must observe the five precepts and practice the ten good deeds.

必須向出家人求戒

持戒就是「諸惡不做，眾善奉行。」戒有多少種呢？有很多種。有五戒－－凡是皈依三寶的人，想往前再進步就要受五戒。受五戒後，再往前進步就是受八戒。受八戒後，再受十戒，那就是沙彌（尼）了。

在家人想求戒，一定要向出家人求。傳戒就是給你戒體，這個給你戒體的人，一定要是比丘。在佛的戒律中，不准比丘尼傳戒的。

PRECEPTS SHOULD BE REQUESTED FROM A LEFT-HOME PERSON—AN ORDAINED MONK

To uphold precepts is just to do no evil but do all good. How many precepts are there? There are many sets of precepts. First, there are the five precepts. Those who have taken refuge with the Triple Jewel and who like to take another step forward should receive the five precepts. After having received the five precepts, another step forward would be to receive the eight precepts. Following that would come the ten precepts for novice monks and nuns.

Lay people who like to receive precepts must request them from an ordained monk. To transmit precepts means to give the precept substance to the preceptees. The person who transmits the precept substance to you must be a Bhikshu. In the Vinaya, a Bhikshuni is not permitted to transmit precepts.

佛教徒要守持的根本戒律

五戒是佛教徒最根本要守的戒律,就是不殺生,不偷盜,不邪婬,不妄語,不飲酒。

不殺生,你常常不殺生就得長壽報,壽命會長。為什麼有的人壽命長?有的人壽命短?壽命長的人,因持不殺戒得長壽報;壽命短的人,因他歡喜殺生就得短命的果報。

為什麼要持不偷戒?因為偷,是損壞人的財產福命。什麼是偷盜?是偷偷

THE BASIC RULES
TO BE OBSERVED BY BUDDHISTS

The five precepts are the most fundamental rules that Buddhists should follow. They are: not killing, not stealing, not engaging in sexual misconduct, not lying and not consuming intoxicants.

If you receive the precept against killing and constantly refrain from killing, you will be rewarded with longevity. You will live a long life. Why is it that some people have long life spans while others have short life spans? Those who had upheld the precept against killing are rewarded with a long life, while people who liked to kill have the retribution of short lives.

Why should we observe the precept against stealing? It is because stealing causes others to lose their wealth. What is stealing? It is covertly taking away properties and materials belonging to others. What's the retri-

的把別人的財產物質偷走了。你儘偷盜別人的東西，你得到什麼果報呢？將來你就受財產不長久的果報。好像你本來很有錢，突然間被強盜搶去了。

婬、妄、酒，也都是這樣子。就好像你不守婬戒，去姦婬別人的婦女，將來你自己的妻女也被人玩弄，這都是一種果報。

妄語，你自己要是不騙人，你就不會被人騙。

說「我這一生沒有騙人，為什麼很多人來騙我呢？」我方才不是說過，這種果報不是一生的事情，是有過去、

bution for stealing others' things? The retribution will be that of not being able to hold one's own wealth long. For example, someone may be rich, and all of a sudden that person gets robbed.

Sexual misconduct, lying, and taking intoxicants are similar. For instance, someone who does not observe the rule against sexual misconduct might have affairs with others' women. In the future, other men will fool arround with that person's own wife or daughter. Those are the kinds of retributions that will happen.

As to lying, if we don't deceive people, we will not be deceived. Someone may complain, "I have never deceived anyone in my life. Why is it that many people deceive me?" Didn't I just say that the matter of retribution is not limited to one lifetime? It spans three time periods: past, present, and future. You may not have cheated anyone in this life, but do you know how many people you have cheated in your previous life? "I don't know." You don't know? So it may be fitting that people cheat you now.

現在、未來,果報是通三世的。你今生沒有騙過人,你可知道你前生你騙過多少人嗎?「我不知道。」你不知道?那有人騙過你,這是應該的。

本來不想說大話,但是總是不假思索就打妄語。這個打妄語很快,不用思索,不用想一想要打什麼妄語。譬如有人問你:「偷東西沒有?你偷了沒有?」就是偷了,你也會說:「我沒有偷。」不用想就說沒有偷。一個「偷」犯了一個戒,「打妄語」又犯了一個戒。

酒飲少是沒有什麼問題,喝多了就會亂性,人就顛倒,所做的事也顛倒,所以佛教裡戒酒。

A person may not have intended to boast, but it's very easy to tell a lie without even realizing it. Telling lies can happen very fast. A lie comes out before we know it. For instance, someone may ask a person, "Have you stolen something?"

The person may reply, "I haven't" without even stopping to think even if he did. If in fact, the person stole, then, by denying it, he commits the offense of lying on top the offense of stealing.

A little wine doesn't hurt. However, if people drink a lot they will become confused and do crazy things. That's why drinking wine is prohibited in Buddhism.

If we were to elaborate, the five precepts encompass many principles. The main point is that when we make sure our hands do no killing, we must also be sure that our minds do not entertain any thoughts of killing. Then we are truly upholding the precept against killing. The same applies to the precept against stealing. When our hands are not stealing, our minds must also be free of thoughts of stealing. Regardless of the value of objects, if someone uses

為什麼要受持五戒？

這五戒說起來是有很多道理。主要的是我們手不去殺生，心裡也不生殺念，這才是真正持「殺戒」。盜也是如此，手不去盜，心也不生盜念。「盜」，不論大小，凡是沒有人許可你，你自己偷偷用了其他人的東西，這都叫犯盜戒。

something or takes something stealthily without getting permission, then that is considered to be a violation of the precept against stealing.

可不可以抽菸?

好像有一個人到外面抽香菸,回來我問他:
「你抽了幾支香菸?」
「我沒有抽啊!」
「有人看見你抽了嘛!他來告訴我的。」
「噢!那...我就抽一個。」

你看,他先是說他沒抽,以後又說抽一個。我說:
「你現在還有幾個?」
「現在還有三個。」
「那七個到哪去了?」

IS SMOKING ALLOWED?

A man went outside to smoke. When he came back, I asked him, "How many cigarettes did you smoke?"

"I didn't smoke." he said.
"Some people saw you." I replied.
"Oh. I smoked one cigarette," he said.

You see. He said he didn't smoke and then said he smoked one cigarette. I said, "How many cigarettes have you got left?"

"Three."
"Where are the other seven?"
"Well..., I don't know."

I picked up a stick and hit him right on the head—Pow! "Do you know what this is? Does it hurt?"

「這...這...I don't know. 我不知道。」我拿一個棍子照他頭就「啪」打一下,「你知不知這是什麼?你覺不覺得痛?」

「覺得痛。」

「你覺得痛,為什麼你要講大話?」

「這...這戒律上沒有說戒菸的。」

「你讀過戒律了嗎?戒律上沒有說戒菸,你一定知道嗎?那個菸就包括在酒裡面。」

「啊!我不知道。」

人抽菸的味道最不好,不單外面的味道不好,就是身裡裡面的味道也不好,尤其是菩薩、善神護法,一發覺你有菸味,就不保護你了。你就是有多大的功德,他也不管你了!你就會遇到很多意外的事情。

"Yes."

"Yes? Then why did you lie?"

"Well...the Vinaya doesn't prohibit smoking."

"Have you studied the Vinaya? Do you know for sure that it doesn't prohibit smoking? Smoking is included in the precept against taking intoxicants."

"Oh! I didn't know."

The smell from smoking is terrible. Not only does it make a person smell bad outside, it also makes the inside of his body smell bad. Bodhisattvas and Dharma-protecting good spirits will not want to protect you when they find out you smell like smoke. No matter how much merit and virtue you may have, they will leave you alone and many accidents will happen to you.

We don't have to talk about others; currently there is one person among us who smoked stealthily and caused a very dangerous incident to occur. It happened because he was smoking, but he still doesn't realize it.

People who smoke will fall into the hell of Flames

不要說別人,我們這兒有一個人偷著抽香菸,所以就遇到很危險的事情,這就是因抽香菸所引起,不過他自己到現在還不知道。

抽香菸的人死了之後,會下火焰地獄。火焰地獄專門給抽菸的人預備的,誰抽菸就有機會去。若是戒了菸,就和火焰地獄斷往還;若不戒,將來就有份的。人不知道這個厲害,就亂來;你知道了就不會做了。抽菸這個問題比喝酒還厲害。

為什麼釋迦牟尼佛沒說戒菸,只說戒酒呢?因為那時候人還不會抽菸,在佛住世時,沒有人懂得抽菸。

after they die. The hell of Flames is especially prepared for smokers. Whoever likes to smoke has the chance to go down there. If you refrain from smoking, you will avoid the path that leads to the hell of Flames. If you don't, however, you may end up there in the future. People do not know the seriousness of such matters and do whatever they like. When you understand, you will not do it. Smoking is a more severe problem then drinking.

Why did Shakyamuni Buddha not prohibit smoking when he prohibited drinking? It is because during that time when the Buddha was in the world no one knew about smoking.

受五戒的重要性

要是能持五戒十善,就能升到天上。
「五戒」--殺、盜、婬、妄、酒。

> 不殺生是慈悲;
> 不偷盜是義氣;
> 不邪婬是正人君子;
> 不妄語是忠信的人;
> 不飲酒是不亂來的人。

> 殺生將來是宿殃短命報;
> 偷盜將來是貧窮苦楚報;
> 邪婬將來是雀鴿鴛鴦報;

小鳥好高騖遠,貪邪婬就做了小鳥。

THE IMPORTANCE OF RECEIVING THE FIVE PRECEPTS

If one can uphold the five precepts and practice the ten good deeds, one will ascend to the heavens. The five precepts are not killing, not stealing, not engaging in sexual misconduct, not lying, and not taking intoxicants.

> *Not killing is being kind and compassionate.*
> *Not stealing is being righteous.*
> *Not engaging in sexual misconduct is being an upright and proper person.*
> *Not lying is being a loyal and faithful person.*
> *Not taking intoxicants is not to be a reckless person.*
>
> *Killing brings the retribution of a short*

為什麼要受持五戒？

我時時跟你們講，你們卻不太注意。我也不怕麻煩，對你們再講一遍。說什麼呢？人不要殺生。因為一切眾生在無量劫以來，和我是親戚，或是朋友，或是父母祖先也不一定的。我們要是殺生的話，前生父母造了罪業，今生托生做牛做豬，我們殺了他們，等於間接殺了我們的父母是一樣的。

再說偷盜，「己所不欲，勿施於人。」自己不願意的事，不要加在別人身上；自己不歡喜的事，不要叫別人做。「不偷盜」，因為我們不願別人偷我們的東西，我們首先就不要偷別人的東西或財物。

至於邪婬，在因果律上，凡是犯邪婬的罪，受的懲罰是很重。尤其夫婦不應該馬馬虎虎隨隨便便離婚，因為你

> life span.
> Stealing brings the retribution of a life of
> poverty and hardship.
> Sexual misconduct brings the retribution of
> being born as pigeons or mandarin ducks.

Birds are impractical and lustful. If people act that way, they will be reborn as birds.

I often tell you these things, but you never pay much attention. I don't mind taking the trouble to remind you again. What is it? People must not kill, because all living beings have either been our relatives or friends, or even parents or ancestors, throughout limitless eons. If our former parents have now been reborn as pigs or cows because of offenses they committed, and we kill those pigs and cows, then that would be the same as killing our own parents indirectly.

As for stealing, it's said, "We should not do to others what we would not like done to us." Since we don't

結婚又離婚,在因果律上,人死後身體要分成兩份。因為你有兩邊的關係,所以用鋸子從頭頂鋸到腳底。你結婚幾次就要分開多少份。一個女人和一百個男人結婚,就分成一百份;一個男人與一百個女人結婚,也要分成一百份。一百個女人,一人分一塊,分得零零碎碎。

分開有什麼不好呢?分了再想把靈性聚集在一起,就很不容易了,這個機會是很不容易得到。得不到這個機會就永遠性化靈殘,與草木同朽,變成無情的植物。因為你的本性分開了,不夠做眾生;就是做眾生,你一個身體要做八萬四千那麼多蚊蟲。這個蚊蟲又去做蚊蟲,總也不知向後轉,不

like having our belongings stolen, we should not steal others' belongings.

In the law of cause and effect, the punishment for sexual misconduct is very heavy. Husbands and wives should not casually divorce. If you are married and then divorce later, in the law of cause and effect, your body will be divided into two parts because you had two relationships. You will be sawed in half from head to toe. You will be sawed into as many pieces as the number of marriages you have had. If a woman married a hundred men, she would be cut into one hundred pieces. Each man would get a piece of her.

What's bad about being cut into fragments? It will be hard for the spiritual nature to come together again. Such a chance would be difficult to come by. If the chance does not arise, the spiritual nature will forever be incomplete and one will become an insentient thing, much like wood or grass. One's nature will be so fragmented that it will be insufficient to function as a sentient being. Even if it does become a sentient being, it would be in the form of a

會背塵合覺,在輪迴裡死了又生,生了又死。

所以「一失人身,萬劫不復。」我們把人的身體失去了,在幾萬個大劫後,也不容易恢復,再得到這個人身。

swarm of eighty-four thousand mosquitoes or the like. Those mosquitoes would in turn become mosquitoes that also lacked any awareness of how to change their course. They would not able to wake up and turn away from the deluded existence. They would continually be born and die within the cycle of transmigration.

Thus, it's said, "Once the human body is lost, it will not be recovered in tens of thousands of eons." If we lose the human body, we will have to pass through millions of eons and still may not be able to regain it.

受五戒的好處

今生不籠鳥，來生不坐監；
今生不釣魚，來生不討飯；
今生不殺生，來生無災難；
今生不偷盜，來生無搶案；
今生不邪婬，來生無婚變；
今生不妄語，來生無欺騙；
今生不醉酒，來生不狂亂。

「今生不籠鳥，來生不坐監」：你想一想，你把鳥關在籠子裡令牠不自由；這個國家是講自由的，你讓畜生不自由，這也不合乎這個國家的憲法。你讓鳥在龍子裡，就和在監獄是一樣，這個鳥就在籠子裡念咒了，說：「果

THE BENEFITS OF RECEIVING
THE FIVE PRECEPTS

Not caging birds in this life, we will not be put in jail in future lives;

Not fishing in this life, we will not become beggars in future lives;

Not killing in this life, we will not encounter difficulties in future lives;

Not stealing in this life, we will not be robbed in future lives;

Not engaging in sexual misconduct in this life, we will have good marriages in future lives;

Not lying in this life, we will not be cheated in future lives;

Not taking intoxicants in this life, we will not

為什麼要受持五戒?

報、果報⋯」來生果報就來了,那個鳥念咒說:「上帝!你說有果報,為什麼他把我放在籠子裡頭?這是怎麼回事?」牠就到玉皇大帝,也就是天主那裡,左寫一張狀子,右寫一張狀子去告狀去。牠寫多了,天主一看:「好了!這個人是不公道,來生也叫他受這個果報。」這個人後來就坐到監獄裡去了。所以說「今生不籠鳥,來生不坐監」,因為那個鳥一天到晚念那個「果報」,念那個「因果報應經」給上帝聽,上帝就判這個人來生去坐監獄。

我記得不是今生,是多少生以前,那時候迷迷糊糊,什麼道理也不懂,看人家釣魚,我也去釣魚,很歡喜釣魚的。看到魚吃魚餌,水就現出一圈圈的波紋,這時把釣魚竿向上一挑,這個魚就釣上來了。你說以後怎麼樣啊?來生就做要飯的,拿個碗向人要

> *lose our sanity in future lives.*
> *"Not caging birds in this life, we will not be put in jail in future lives."*

Think about it. When someone puts a bird in a cage, he takes its freedom away. By doing that, the person is not abiding by the constitution of this country. This country advocates freedom. Caging a bird is the same as putting the bird behind bars. The bird will start chanting the mantra, "retribution, retribution…" In the future, the bird will go before the Jade Emperor, who is the Lord of the Heavens, and file a suit against the person who caged it.

The Heavenly Lord will say, "Okay, this person has not been fair. He shall undergo the retribution!" You will then go to jail in future lives. This is because the bird has been chanting the mantra of retribution from morning to night. When the Heavenly Lord hears it, his verdict is that the person who caged the bird should be put behind bars.

I recall how not in this life but in some other life in the past, I was deluded and didn't know any better. I

飯，因為沒有東西吃。所以說「今生不釣魚，來生不討飯。」要飯是很苦的，儘向人討飯吃，所以我們信佛的人少釣點魚是好的。

有人說：「我少釣點魚可以，一年釣一次；我只釣小魚，不釣大魚，這樣好不好呢？」小魚也是一條命，大魚也是一條命；你釣一次也是殺生，你釣多次也是殺生。不過你釣的少，欠的債會少一點；釣的多，欠的債也就多一點：也就是你釣半斤，將來要還八兩。

「今生不殺生，來生無災難」：你今生不殺一切的生靈，等來生就沒有人殺你，也沒有一切的災難，也不會被槍打死，也不會火燒死，也不會被水淹死。因為你前生沒有殺生，今生也就沒有病痛。

saw people fishing so I went fishing too. I was quite fond of doing it. When the fish took the bait the water rippled. Then I would swing the fishing pole upward and the fish would be hooked. What happened to me afterward? I became a beggar in the next life. I had to beg for food because I didn't have anything to eat. Thus, it's said, "*Not fishing in this life, we will not become beggars in future lives.*" It's quite miserable to beg for food. It's better that we Buddhists do less fishing.

Someone may say, "I can do less fishing. I'll fish just once a year. And I will only fish for small and not big fish. Will that be okay?" Well, a small fish is a life, just the same as a big fish. Fishing once a year, you still end up killing, just the same as when you fish many times a year. However, if you fish less, your debt will be less; fish more, and your debt will be greater. That is to say, if you catch half a pound of fish, you must pay back eight ounces in the future.

Not killing in this life, we will not encounter difficulties in future lives. If you refrain from killing any living being, then in future lives you will not be killed and

「今生不偷盜,來生無搶案」:搶案就是你打劫我,我打劫你。你若不偷盜別人的東西,來生沒有人搶劫你的東西。為什麼有人搶你的東西?就因為你前生偷盜,以為偷盜是不錯的,把別人的東西偷回來,到今生別人又把它搶回去。所以這個因果循環是很不可思議的。

「今生不邪婬,來生不婚變」:什麼叫婚變呢?譬如離婚,或者結婚後有很多麻煩,這都因為前生不守戒律,有邪婬的行為,今生身體上還有一種狐臭味,很大的。你怎樣搽香水塗香粉,還是臭的,臭不可聞。本來男人都喜歡女人,但是一聞這個味道都熏跑了;本來女人也都喜歡男人的,但是這個男人有這股臭氣,把女人都熏跑了,所以沒有人會愛你的。因為不持戒律,身上沒有香氣;你要是持戒

you will be free from all difficulties. You will not be shot to death, burned to death, or drowned. Since you didn't kill in previous lives, you will also be free from all illnesses in this life.

Not stealing in this life, we will not be robbed in future lives. If you don't rob others of their things, no one will rob you in future lives. Why would you get robbed? It would happen because you had robbed people in previous lives. You thought it was quite clever to steal others' belongings. This life, they snatch things back. The cycle of cause and effect is quite inconceivable.

Not engaging in sexual misconduct in this life, we will have good marriages in future lives. What is a good marriage? It means there will be no divorce or any other marital troubles. Divorce and marital troubles are a result of failure to follow precepts. Those who have engaged in sexual misconduct will be born with a bad body odor. Whoever did not observe precepts, will have a very bad body smell in this life. The smell will be so strong that no perfume will be able to cover it. Men usually like women, but when they smell that

律,戒律精嚴,你的身體就會放一股香氣,香光莊嚴。

你看在中國清朝的香妃,大概是維吾爾的民族,是回子那邊的人。她身上總是放香的,不用搽香水或用香皂,她身上自然有股香氣,比什麼都香。所以中國那個糊塗皇帝,就歡喜身上放香的女人,就去出征把她搶回來,封她叫「香妃」,令其他的女人妒嫉她。因為皇帝有很多老婆,三宮六院,這個正宮娘娘妒嫉她,就把她殺死了,這個香妃也就不香了。

今生不邪婬,你很守規矩不跟別的女人或男人去邪婬,來生你結婚也不會離婚的。因為你前生不忠實,今生也搞得不愉快,有種種特別因緣就婚變。婚姻有變故了,這是邪婬的果報。

odor, they will run away. Women are also fond of men, but if a man has such a smell, women will also run away from him. Such a person will not be loved. Anyone who does not uphold precepts will not smell good. If you uphold precepts in earnest, your body will emit a fragrance and will be said to be "adorned with fragrant light."

The court lady Madame Fragrance of Chin Dynasty in China, probably a member of the Uighurs, always emitted a fragrance. She didn't have to use perfume or scented soap. She had this natural fragrance from her body that was more fragrant than anything else. The deluded Chinese emperor waged a war and took her back. He named her "Madame Fragrance," which made all of his other women jealous. The emperor had many wives, and his jealous empress had her killed, after which she was no longer fragrant.

In this life, if you do not engage in sexual misconduct by having affairs, you will not divorce in future lives. But if you were not faithful in previous lives, your marriage in this life will not be a happy one. Various things will happen to disrupt your marriage.

為什麼要受持五戒？

「今生不妄語，來生無欺騙」：因為今生不打妄語，到來生沒有人會欺騙你。所以有人欺騙自己，「噢！原來前生自己打過妄語，所以今生才有人欺騙我。」有人告訴我，從菲律賓來的四個人不是真的要來出家，是想藉這條路來這裡，來了以後不會出家。我說沒有關係，我就是明明知道他們是欺騙我，我還是相信他們。因為我不願意欺騙人，我也相信人不欺騙我。我明明知道他是欺騙我，我也不想他是欺騙我，我不這麼想。那個人聽了之後說：「噢！這是好的！」這個世界就是你防備我，我防備你；你怕我欺騙你，我怕你欺騙我。那我知道他欺騙我，卻不這麼想，是不是吃虧了？吃虧就吃虧了，沒有關係。

「今生不醉酒，來生不狂亂」：來生就不會發癲狂，發神經。為什麼你今生

That is the retribution for engaging in sexual misconduct.

Not lying in this life, we will not be cheated in future lives. If we don't lie in this life, no one will cheat us in future lives. If someone cheats us, we must realize, "Oh, I must have lied in a previous life and so I am being cheated in this life."

Someone told me that the four people from the Philippines did not come to leave the home-life. They just used that as an excuse to come to the United States I said that it's all right. I know their motive very clearly, but I still believe them because I don't want to cheat people and I also believe that people will not deceive me. Even if I know someone is cheating me, I will not bring forth the thought that he is. Those people may hear me and say, "Oh! That's good." In this world, many people put up defensive fronts against each other. You fear that I may cheat you, and I am afraid that you may deceive me. Am I taking a loss by not minding being cheated? If I am, it doesn't matter.

發神經,精神不正常?就因為你前生喝酒喝得太多了。那個麻醉藥、迷幻藥也吃了很多,所以到今生狂性還不斷。這個因果循環就是這樣的。信不信由你,我不管。你信,我也這麼說;你不信,我也這麼說:不管你信不信,我都要說。

Not drinking in this life, we will not lose our sanity in future lives. Why is it that people lose their sanity or have mental illness in this life? It is because they drank too much and took a lot of drugs in previous lives. Therefore, the insanity continues into this life. The circular flow of cause and effect is this way whether you believe it or not. Whether you believe it or not I will say it just the same.

學佛法沒有什麼利益？

「唉！我學習佛法，研究佛法，聽經聞法，已經有這麼長的時間了，我還沒有得道什麼利益！」你想得到什麼利益？其實這個利益對你是很大的，你卻不知道。什麼利益呢？

譬如你在這裡學習佛法，你就不會去殺人，在殺人罪犯裡就沒有你了。你說這不是好處嗎？你這兒聽經聞法，偷盜的罪犯裡又沒有你了；你若不聽經聞法，說不定就偷盜、殺人、放火，偷盜的罪犯裡，你恐怕就有一份了。你說這不是好處嗎？

IS THERE NO BENEFIT IN STUDYING THE BUDDHADHARMA?

"I have studied, investigated, and listened to the Buddhadharma for a long, long time and I have not gained any benefit!" What benefit do you want? In fact, you have gained great benefit without knowing it. What kind of benefit have you gained?

When you study Buddhadharma here, you aren't out murdering people. Therefore, you are not among those murderers. Is that not a benefit? When you come here to attend Dharma lectures, you will not be found among thieves and burglars. If you don't listen to lectures, you may get involved in theft, robbery, or even arson. Now that you study Buddhadharma, you are free from all these crimes. Wouldn't you say that's a benefit?

When learning Buddhadharma, you do not get involved in sexual misconduct. so you won't commit

為什麼要受持五戒？

你現在學習佛法，身就不會去犯婬業，不會到外面去行婬欲。你沒有這種行為，在姦殺的罪犯裡又沒有你這一份了。你做很多正當的事，這個罪犯裡你有沒有份了。這豈不是好處呢？你在這兒學佛法不會去打妄語，不會去外面欺騙人，那麼打妄語的罪犯裡又沒有你了。你這就是口業清淨了。你再不喝酒，不抽菸，不吸毒，不吃種種迷魂藥了，你的意業也會清淨了，就會不貪，不瞋，不癡，因為你不吃那些迷人的東西，所以吸毒罪犯裡面你也沒有一份了。

這三業清淨不是學佛法的好處是什麼？你如果不學佛法，殺人、放火、偷東西，警察就會捉你坐監。甚至讓你永遠不能出來，你說這是苦不苦？你學佛法，把這些的災難都沒有了。這不是好處是什麼？所以要心無疲厭，常常來學佛法。

crimes such as rape. You do many proper things so you will be free from all crimes. Isn't that a benefit? When you study Buddhadharma, you won't tell lies or go around cheating people. Then, you won't commit the offense of lying. That is purifying your mouth karma. If you can further refrain from drinking, smoking, and taking drugs, then your mind karma will be purified too. Since you don't consume those intoxicants, you won't be in the company of criminal addicts either.

If purifying the three karmas is not a benefit of learning Buddhism, then what is it? If you don't study the Buddhadharma, you may kill, or steal, or get involved in arson. Then the police will catch you and put you behind the bars, perhaps for life. Wouldn't that be miserable? Since you are studying the Buddhadharma, you are free from all these problems. If that is not a benefit, what is it then? Therefore, we should not grow weary of studying the Buddhadharma.

不受戒是真「自由」嗎？

有邪知邪見的人說：「不要受戒。你受戒做什麼？何必弄個『戒』來管著你？不受戒多自由呢！你何必要受戒呀？」你以為不受戒是自由，卻很容易墮地獄了。那真是「自由」，很容易就跑到地獄去了。

你若受戒，有戒來支持你，有戒相、戒法、戒體支持你，就不容易墮地獄；就是墮地獄也很快就出來了。你要是聽其自由不受戒，以後墮落地獄裡，什麼時候才能出來，那是沒有人能擔保的。

WILL NOT RECEIVING PRECEPTS GIVE YOU TRUE FREEDOM?

People with wrong views say, "Don't take the precepts. What do you want to take them for? Why get some precepts to restrain you?" That is a wrong view. You think that not receiving the precepts is being free. But it's very easy to fall into the hells that way. That's where your so-called "true freedom" may lead you. If you receive the precepts, you will have the protection of the precepts. The precept mark, precept dharma, and precept substance will support you. You will not fall into the hells that easily. Even if you do fall into the hells, you will get out quickly. If you like to be free and don't take the precepts, then later when you fall into the hells, it's not for sure when you will come out.

If you have received the precepts, then you will have the precept mark, the precept dharma, and the precept substance to protect you. With this protection your time span in the hells can be shortened. If you

為什麼要受持五戒？

你要是受過戒，墮地獄的時間，由很長的時間可以縮短。好像你犯了很大的法，被警察捉住，因為你給總統做護衛、茶房，總統就寫字條叫人把你放出來，你很快就出來了。若是沒有這種關係，很久的時間也不能放出來，不知要拖延多久，這是同一個道理。你有「戒」來保護你，它可以把你受很長罪的時間，縮為很短的時間。所以不要自作聰明，說不受戒是好的。

你們受戒，這是好的。我告訴你們，眾生受佛戒，即入諸佛位。眾生受了佛戒，就是入了佛位，所以不要譭佛禁戒，不要譭謗佛的戒律。

Why should we receive and uphold the Five Precepts?

let yourself run free and don't receive the precepts, then it is not for certain how long you will have to stay in the hells once you fall into them.

On the other hand, if you have received the precepts your time span in the hells can be shortened. It is like when someone who committed a major crime gets caught by the police. If the criminal had worked as a personal guard or an attendant for the president, then the president may write a note ordering that criminal's release. If the criminal doesn't have such a connection, he won't be released for who knows how long. It is similar to that. When you have the protection of precepts, the long duration of your suffering can be greatly condensed. Therefore, don't get smart and say, "It's good not to receive the precepts."

It's good for you to receive the precepts. Let me say this to you, "Having taken the Buddha's precepts, living beings enter the position of all Buddhas." When living beings take the precepts of the Buddhas, it's the same as having entered the position of the Buddha. Therefore, don't disparage the precepts or slander the Vinaya of the Buddha.

學佛法就要學戒、定、慧。

戒,就是「諸惡不作,眾善奉行。」凡是惡的事都不要做;一切的善事都要做。

定,就是勤修禪定。慧,就是由戒生定,由定發慧。這是戒定慧三無漏學。

要息滅貪、瞋、癡,要不貪、不瞋、不癡;沒有貪了就不爭了,不爭了就無所求了。你無所求就不自私了,不自私也就不自利了,所以這都有連帶的關係。學佛法就是要老老實實照這個方法做去,不能投機走捷徑,躐等而進,要這樣子實實在在去修行。

IN LEARNING BUDDHADHARMA, WE MUST LEARN PRECEPTS, CONCENTRATION, AND WISDOM.

Precepts help us to "refrain from all evil and do all good." We refrain from doing whatever is bad, but we do all good things. Concentration is the vigorous study of chan meditation. Wisdom is the result of concentration, and concentration comes from upholding precepts. These are called the three non-outflow studies.

We must put an end to greed, hatred and delusion. Being free from greed, we will not fight. When we do not fight with others, we seek nothing. When we do not seek, we will be selfless. When we are selfless, we will not pursue personal advantage. All these are related. Studying Buddhadharma means following the teaching in a precise and honest manner. Don't take chances and shortcuts, just cultivate honestly.

老修行的故事

以前有個老修行,是在家人不是出家人。他受了五戒,另外又受了一個「食不語」的戒。可是他把五戒都犯了,就剩這個「食不語」的戒未犯。護這條戒的戒神就希望他快點犯這條戒,他也好走了,不保護他。但是這個人始終也不犯這條戒,吃飯的時候,他總不講話。以後這個戒神就給他托夢:「你什麼戒都犯了,為什麼吃飯這個戒你不犯呢?你快點犯,我好離開你了。」

THE STORY OF AN OLD CULTIVATOR

Once an old lay cultivator had received the five precepts and an additional rule of keeping silent while eating. However, later he broke all five precepts and only kept the rule of keeping silent while eating. The precept-protecting spirit that protected this rule hoped that the lay man would violate it so that he could also leave. This man, nonetheless, never broke that rule. He always ate in silence.

Later, that precept spirit appeared in a dream, "You have transgressed all the precepts. Why haven't you broken this rule of keeping silent while eating? Please break it quickly so I can leave."

The old cultivator thought to himself, "I only hold this one rule of eating in silence and still I have that precept spirit protecting me." Thereafter, he found

這個老修行心想:「噢!我就持一個食不語的戒,果然有戒神保護著我。」於是他後來又找了一個有道德的法師,又重受過戒,結果他也修行成道了!這每一個人有每一個人的因緣。

所以受戒在佛教裡是很重要的事。

a virtuous Dharma Master and received the five precepts again. Consequently, he cultivated and realized the Way. Each person has his own set of causes and conditions.

Therefore, receiving precepts is a very important matter in Buddhism.

文殊菩薩的寶珠

文殊師利這位菩薩修菩薩行時不打妄語,也不殺生也不偷盜。總而言之,他謹守戒律。由什麼證明他守戒律而不偷盜呢?他有一次對其他的菩薩講:「我從一發心修行就持不盜戒,所以現在我所有的東西就沒有人偷盜;不單沒有人偷盜,我就是把最值錢的東西放在地上,也沒有人會把它拿去。」

有的菩薩就不信他的話,就說:「我們要有實地的試驗,實實在在地試驗一下。你把你最值錢的東西拿出來,我

MAÑJUŚRĪ BODHISATTVA'S
PRECIOUS PEARL

While Mañjuśrī Bodhisattva was practicing the Bodhisattva Way, he never lied. Nor did he commit any offense involving killing or stealing. In general, he upheld the precepts strictly. How can we prove that he followed those rules and never stole things? Once, he told the other Bodhisattvas, "Ever since my initial resolve to cultivate, I have held the rule of not stealing. Therefore, my belongings will not be stolen by anyone. Not only will no one steal from me, even if I leave my most valuable possession out in the open, no one will walk away with it."

Some Bodhisattvas didn't believe him and said, "We would like to test your claim with an experiment. Leave your most valuable thing at the city gate, which is the busiest place. Leave it there for three days. If

們把它放在城門那個地方,因為那兒來回走的人最多了。我們把它放在門的中間,經過三天,如果沒有人拿這個東西,這證明你說的是實在的。」

文殊師利菩薩說:「好啊!我們就來試試看!」於是他把他最值錢的一個寶珠拿出來--菩薩都有很多寶貝寶珠的--就放在城門的中間。人從城外進到城裡來,經過這個城門的人很多,可是經過三天,果然沒有人拿。所以一般的菩薩都知道文殊師利菩薩守不盜戒是真的。

no one picks it up, that will prove that your statement is true."

Mañjuśrī Bodhisattva agreed to the experiment. Thereupon, he put his most precious pearl—all Bodhisattvas possess many precious and valuable things—at the city gate. Many people passed through the gate in the next three days and sure enough, no one picked it up. The other Bodhisattvas then knew that Mañjuśrī Bodhisattva had truly upheld the precept against stealing.

不要做自己的辯護律師

一樣的佛法,每一個人的講法不同,修行法不同,每一個人的見解不同,所以有很多種類的分別,又有很多種類的看法。

譬如真正修佛法的人,要不抽菸不喝酒,不吃那麼多的肉。有的同是佛教裡面的人就說了:「佛講戒律教人不殺生,不偷盜,不邪婬,不妄語,不喝酒,沒有叫人不抽菸,所以抽菸不在佛教的戒律以內。」這就是自己給自己講道理。根本抽菸的問題就在飲酒裡面,不過自己要給自己做辯護律師,就說抽菸是不犯戒的。

DON'T ACT AS YOUR OWN DEFENSE ATTORNEY

Different people explain the same Buddhadharma in many different ways. Accordingly, the methods of cultivation are also different. Each person has his own interpretation. Therefore, there are many different viewpoints.

For instance, true cultivators of Buddhadharma should not smoke, drink, or eat meat. But some Buddhists say, "The Buddha's precepts prohibit people from killing, stealing, indulging in sexual misconduct, lying, or drinking. However, there's no mention of smoking. Therefore, smoking is not included in the precepts." This is a self-justification. Smoking is covered in the precept against drinking. People want to act as their own defense attorneys so they say smoking is not a violation of the precepts.

為什麼要受持五戒？

真正有智慧的人，凡是不對的事情都應該不做，也不一定要佛講戒律講到這個問題，我才不做；沒說到我就要做，不是這樣的。一切惡劣的習慣，我們都應該改了它。

我們說不吃肉，不殺生，這個不殺生也包括了不吃肉；這個不吃肉也包括了不殺生，因為你要不殺生就沒有肉吃了。有的佛教徒又說了：「佛沒教人不吃肉，只是教人不殺生。佛都允許人吃三淨肉－－不見殺，不聞殺，不為我殺；吃三淨肉是可以的。」這也是自己口裡饞，捨不得這個肉味，所以這樣辯護。

以前我遇到一個教授，一天不吃肉也不行的，一定要吃肉。他說：「我即使不吃肉，就是聞聞肉味也是好的，都解饞了。」所以你看，每個人的見解是不同的，各人有各人的思想。

A person with true wisdom will not do anything improper. He will refrain from doing any manner of bad things, not just those mentioned in the precepts. We should change all our bad habits.

Not killing includes not eating meat and not eating meat also includes not killing. That is because if we don't kill, there will be no meat to eat. Some Buddhists say, "The Buddha prohibited people from killing, but not from eating meat. The Buddha allowed people to eat the meat that is pure in three ways: 1) One does not see the creature killed; 2) one does not hear the creature being killed; 3) the creature was not killed especially for oneself. Eating meat that is pure in these ways is permitted." That is also a self-justification because such a person basically can not renounce meat.

I met a professor once who could not get by for a single day without eating meat. He said, "Even the smell of meat would relieve my craving for it if I couldn't get to taste it." So you see, each person has his own ideas and views and they are all different.

什麼是淨戒？

各位要注意這個「淨」字。淨,是什麼意思呢?就是不染污,就是清淨,絲毫的染污也沒有,這種淨就是一念不生謂之淨,淨念。

你單在外邊持戒,說:「我不殺生。」你心裡常常不滿意人,或者發人的脾氣,這都犯殺戒了。

偷盜,你不必真正去偷去,就心裡面羨慕人家的財物或者技能,妒嫉人,這都犯了盜戒了。

WHAT ARE PURE PRECEPTS?

You should pay attention to the word "pure." What does "pure" mean? It means being pure and clean, free from all defilement. Not having the slightest defilement is the kind of purity in which not even a single thought arises.

Not killing includes purifying our thoughts. If we uphold precepts on the surface and claim that we don't kill, but we complain about others constantly or get angry with people, we are still violating the precept against killing.

Not stealing includes mental states. We don't have to steal physically. When we envy others' wealth or talents, or become jealous of people, we transgress the precept against stealing.

邪婬,你心裡儘打異性的妄想,這都叫犯了婬,都是不淨了。

這個淨戒,就要乾乾淨淨的,一點染污念也沒有了,這才是淨戒。

Not committing sexual misconduct includes not having improper thoughts about the opposite sex. If we indulge in improper thoughts about the opposite sex, then we are being impure and breaking the precept.

Holding the precepts purely means leading a clean life without any defiled thoughts. That is to hold the precepts purely.

迴向偈

願以此功德　　莊嚴佛淨土
上報四重恩　　下濟三塗苦
若有見聞者　　悉發菩提心
盡此一報身　　同生極樂國

VERSE OF TRANSFERENCE

May the merit and virtue accrued from this work
Adorn the Buddhas' Pure Lands,
Repaying four kinds of kindness above
And aiding those suffering in the paths below.
May those who see and hear of this
All bring forth the resolve for Bodhi
And, when this retribution body is over,
Be born together in the Land of Ultimate Bliss.

南無護法韋陀菩薩

NAMO DHARMA PROTECTOR
WEI TUO BODHISATTVA

法界佛教總會 · 萬佛聖城
Dharma Realm Buddhist Association
The City of Ten Thousand Buddhas
P.O. Box 217, 2001 Talmage Road, Talmage, CA 95481-0217 U.S.A.
Tel: (707) 462-0939   Fax: (707) 462-0949   http://www.drba.org

法界聖城 The City of the Dharma Realm
1029 West Capitol Avenue, West Sacramento, CA 95691 U.S.A.
Tel/Fax: (916) 374-8268

金山聖寺 Gold Mountain Monastery
800 Sacramento Street, San Francisco, CA 94108 U.S.A.
Tel: (415) 421-9112   Fax: (415) 788-6001

國際譯經學院 The International Translation Institute
1777 Murchison Drive, Burlingame, CA 94010-4504 U.S.A.
Tel: (650) 692-5912   Fax: (650) 692-5056

法界宗教研究院（柏克萊寺）
Institute for World Religions (at Berkeley Buddhist Monastery)
2304 McKinley Avenue, Berkeley, CA 94703 U.S.A.
Tel: (510) 848-3440   Fax: (510) 548-4551

金聖寺 Gold Sage Monastery
11455 Clayton Road, San Jose, CA 95127 U.S.A.
Tel: (408) 923-7243   Fax: (408) 923-1064

金輪聖寺 Gold Wheel Monastery
235 North Avenue 58, Los Angeles, CA 90042 U.S.A.
Tel/Fax: (323) 258-6668

長堤聖寺 Long Beach Monastery
3361 East Ocean Boulevard, Long Beach, CA 90803 U.S.A.
Tel/Fax: (562) 438-8902

福祿壽聖寺 Blessings, Prosperity, and Longevity Monastery
4140 Long Beach Boulevard, Long Beach, CA 90807 U.S.A.
Tel/Fax: (562) 595-4966

華嚴精舍 Avatamsaka Hermitage
11721 Beall Mountain Road, Potomac, MD 20854-1128 U.S.A.
Tel/Fax: (301) 299-3693

金峰聖寺 Gold Summit Monastery
233 First Avenue West, Seattle, WA 98119 U.S.A.
Tel/Fax: (206) 284-6690